READ~ALOUD BIBLE STORIES

VOL. 3

Ella K. Lindvall

ILLUSTRATED BY

H. Kent Puckett

MOODY PRESS
CHICAGO

Once again, for Jason

Moody Press, a ministry of the Moody Bible Insti-
tute, is designed for education, evangelization, and
edification. If we may assist you in knowing more
about Christ and the Christian life, please write us
without obligation: Moody Press, c/o MLM, Chicago,
Illinois 60610.

Contents

How God Made the World
(Genesis 1:1-27, 31; 2:7, 18-22; 3:20)

Do you like to make things?
God likes to make things.
It was God who made the world.

God said, "Come, light!"
And the dark ran away.
God said, "That's good."
He called the light DAY.
He called the dark NIGHT.

Then God said,
"Come, sky!"
and the sky came.
Next God said,

"Come, dry land!"
Up came the big hills.
Up came the little hills.
Down ran the water
into God's place for it.
God said, "That's good."
Then God said,

"Come, plants!"
Up grew the apple trees.
Up grew the corn.
Up grew the beans.
Up grew the green grass.
God said, "That's good."
Then He said,

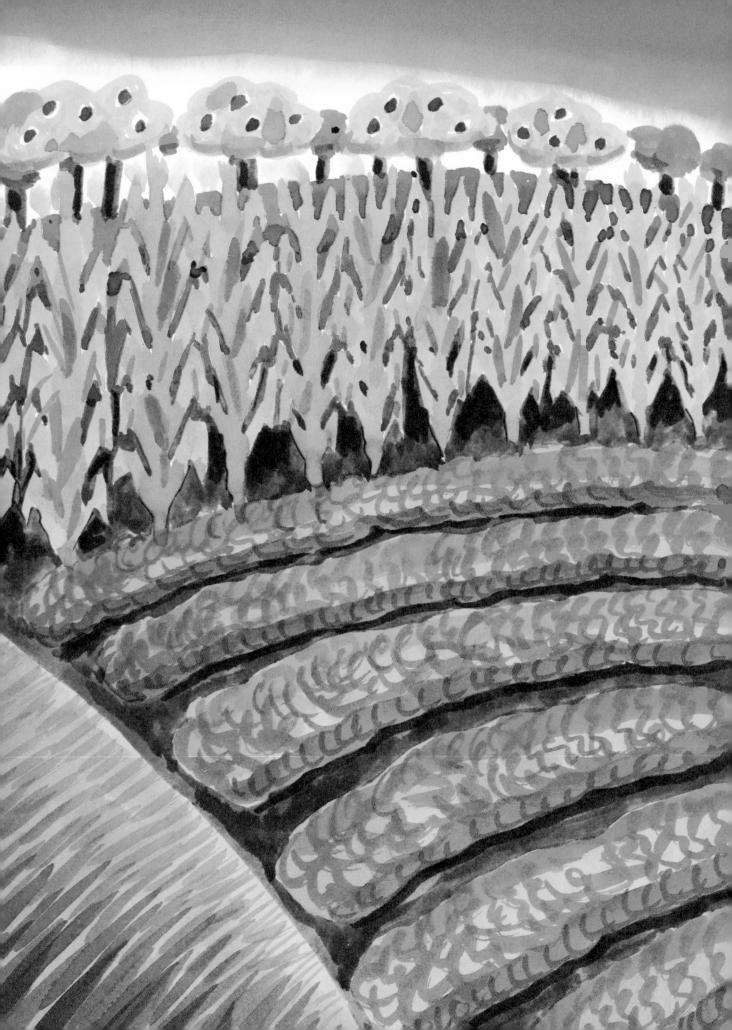

"Come, sun!
Come, moon!
Shine in the sky!"
(He made the stars too.)
God said, "That's good."
Then He said,

"Come, fish!
Come, birds!"
God made the big fish.
God made the little fish.
God made the big birds.
God made the little birds.
God said, "That's good."
Then He said,

"Come, animals!"
God made the cats.
God made the dogs.
God made the horses.
God made the lions.
God made the bears.

God made the bunnies.
God made the butterflies.
God made the wiggily worms.
God made them all.
Then He said,

"Now let's make PEOPLE!"
First, God made a daddy.
His name was Adam.

God brought His animals
to Adam.
Adam said, "Your name
will be dog.
And your name will be cat.
Your name will be horse.
Your name will be lion."
He gave a name
to every one.

Last of all,
God made a beautiful mommy.
God brought her to Adam.
And Adam was very pleased.
Adam said,
"Her name will be Eve."

Then God looked
at all He had made—
day and night,
sky and water,
land and plants,
sun and moon,
shiny stars,
fish and birds,
animals and
PEOPLE.

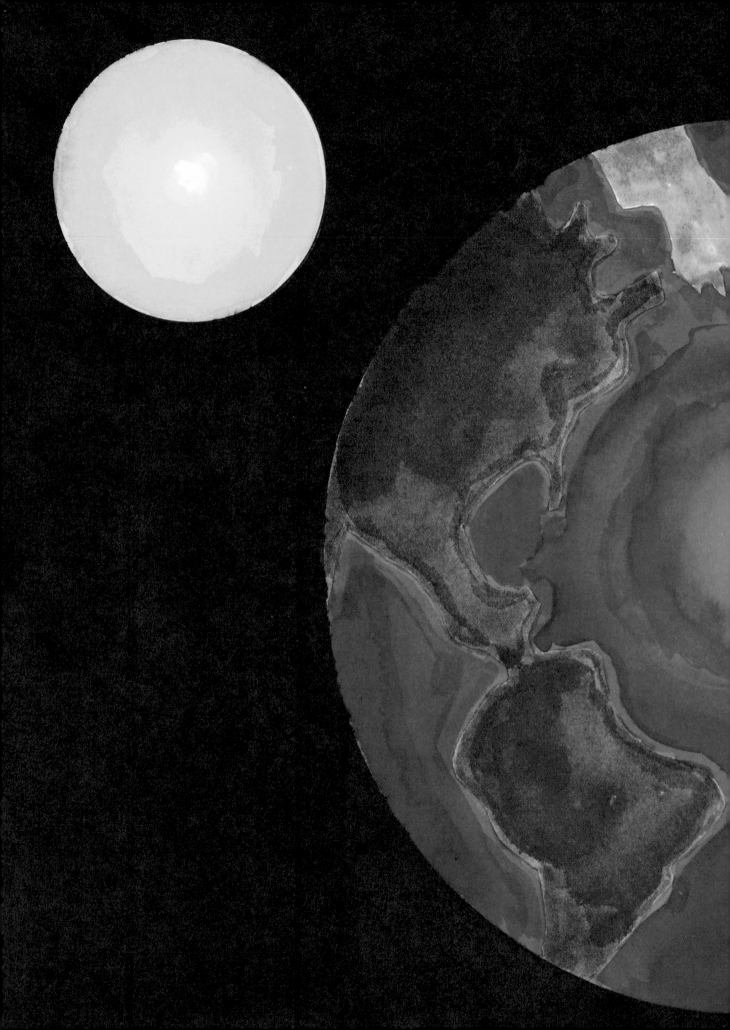

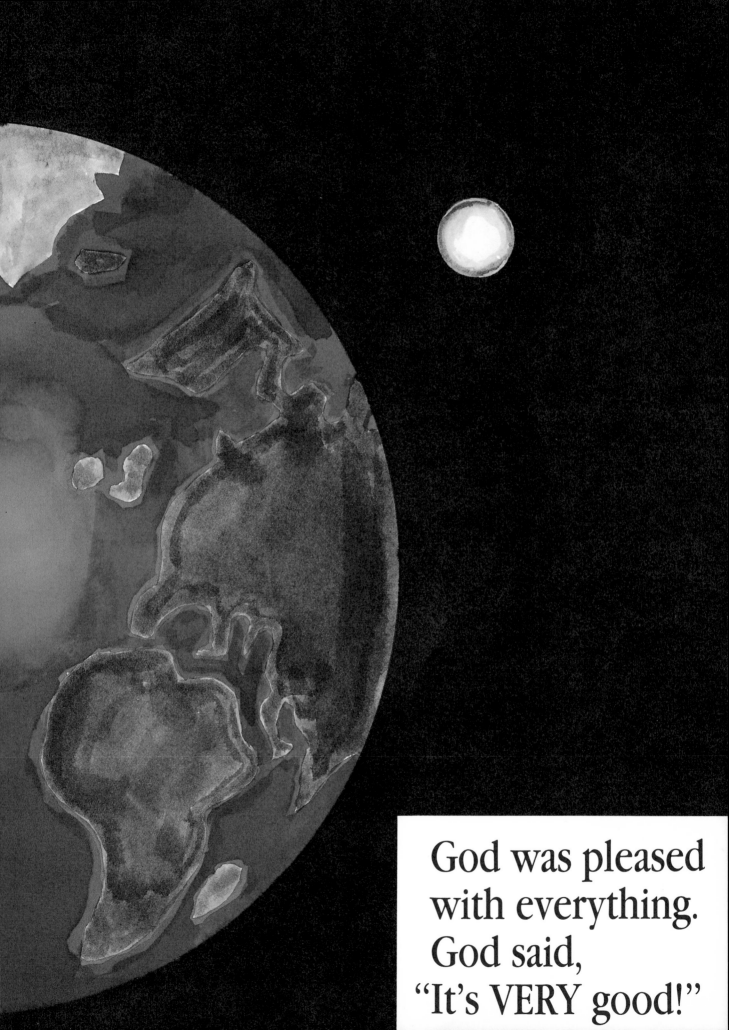

God was pleased with everything. God said, "It's VERY good!"

What did you learn?

God did it.
It was God
who made everything.
And He made everything
JUST RIGHT.

Noah's Big Boat
(Genesis 6:5–9:16)

Noah was God's friend.
Noah made God happy.
Noah tried to do
just what God told him.

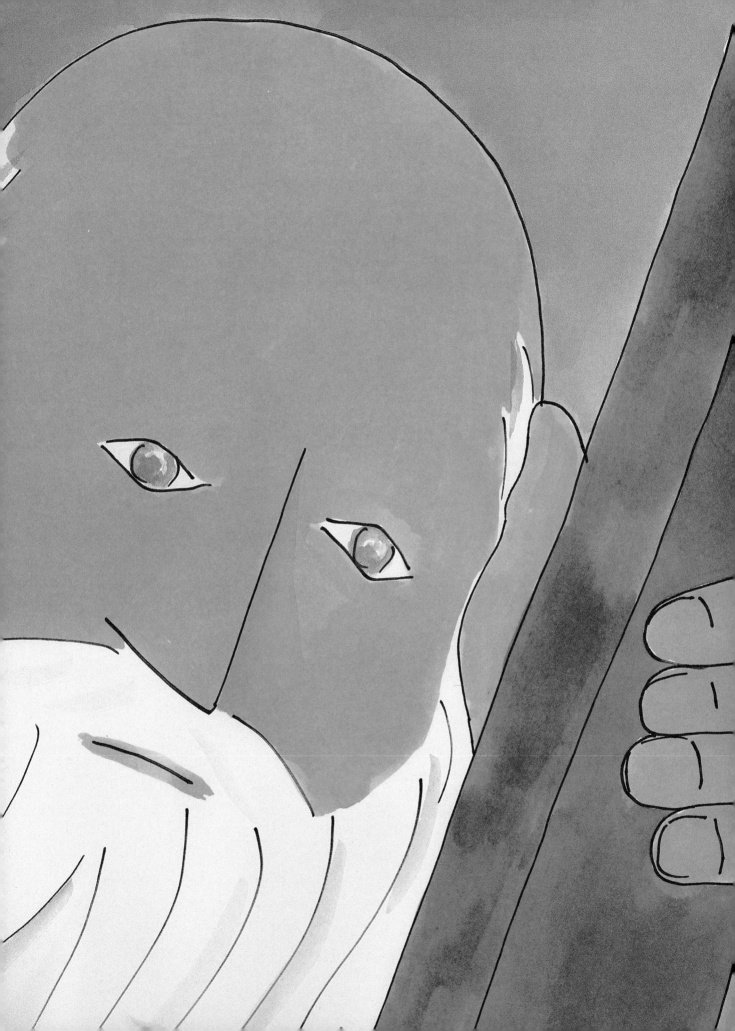

Now Noah had three boys.
Their names were Shem
and Ham and Japheth.

God said, "Noah,
make a big houseboat.
Water is coming.
Water will cover up
everything.
You will be safe on the boat."
And Noah did what God told him.

God said, "Make rooms in the boat."
Noah made rooms.
God said, "Make a window in the boat."
Noah made a window.
God said, "Make a door in the boat."
Noah made a door.

God said, "Put something
to eat
on the boat."
Noah did
what God told him.
God said,
"Put animals
on the boat."
Noah did
what God told him.
Into the houseboat went—

Mr. and Mrs. Cat,
Mr. and Mrs. Horse,
Mr. and Mrs. Dog,
Mr. and Mrs. Pig,
Mr. and Mrs. Grasshopper,
Mr. and Mrs. Wooly Worm,
Mr. and Mrs. Duck,
and more animals too.
Then God said,

"Now you and your family get on the boat."
So Mr. and Mrs. Noah got on the boat.
Mr. and Mrs. Shem got on the boat.
Mr. and Mrs. Ham got on the boat.
Mr. and Mrs. Japheth got on the boat.
And THEN

God shut the door.
After a while,
down came the rain,
DRIP, DRIP, DRIP.
After a while,
up came the water,
SPLASH, SPLASH, SPLASH.
Soon—

water ran over the streets.
Water ran over the houses.
Water ran over the little hills.
Water ran over the big hills.

Now the houseboat was floating!
But Noah was safe inside.
His family was safe inside.
The animals were safe inside.

Noah's family
had something to eat.
They gave the animals
something to eat.
Then they waited.
They waited till the water
went away.
They waited till God said,
"IT'S TIME TO GET OFF
THE BOAT."

Noah did
what God told him.
Mr. and Mrs. Noah
got off the boat.
Mr. and Mrs. Shem
got off the boat.
Mr. and Mrs. Ham
got off the boat.
Mr. and Mrs. Japheth
got off the boat.

All the animals
got off the boat.
They walked and ran
and crawled and hopped.
God said,

"Don't worry.
The water won't come back.
The water won't cover up
the world anymore."
(It never has.)
And God made a rainbow.

What did you learn?

Noah did just what God said.
God took care of Noah.
God takes care
of all the mommies and daddies
and boys and girls
who do what He says.
You too.

God Gives His People Bread to Eat
(Exodus 16:1-18, 3l; Numbers 11:7-8)

STEP. STEP. STEP.
STEP. STEP. STEP.
Moses was taking
the people
on a long walk.

STEP. STEP. STEP.
Every day
the people walked.
Every day
they stopped to eat.
Every night
they stopped to sleep.

One day they came
to an empty place.
It was time to eat,
but their bread
was all gone.
Oh, my.

Now God knew
His people were hungry.
God said to Moses,
"Don't worry.
I will give you bread
from heaven to eat."

So Moses said,
"Don't worry.
God will give you
all the bread you need."

Next morning
the boys and girls
woke up.
The mommies and daddies
woke up.
The grandmas and grandpas
woke up.
The aunts and uncles
and friends
woke up.

They saw something on the ground.
It was little and round and white.
They said, "Oh, look! What is it?"

Moses told them,
"This is the bread
that God has given you."

They called the bread "manna."
They put it in their baskets.
The boys and girls helped.
And THEN—

the mommies
and grandmas
and aunts
cooked the manna.
They made little cakes with it.
The cakes tasted
like bread and honey.
Mmmm, good.

Everybody had manna
for breakfast
and for lunch
and for dinner.
Now NOBODY was hungry.
And the next morning—

God gave them some more.

What did you learn?

God knew His people were hungry.
He gave them something to eat.
He has made good things
for us to eat too.
Can you think of some?

Daniel and the Lions
(Daniel 6:1-23)

Daniel was the king's helper.
Daniel was the king's friend.
Daniel was God's friend, too.
He talked to God every day.

One day the king said,
"EVERYBODY STOP PRAYING!
You must pray just to ME!
If you pray to God,
I'll put you where the lions are!"

Now Daniel heard
what the king said.
Daniel thought
about the lions.
Daniel said,
"I will pray to God anyway."
So—

Daniel went home.
He went upstairs.
He got down on his knees.
And he talked to God.

The next day
Daniel talked to God again.
Soon the king's men came.
They saw Daniel praying,
and they ran to tell the king.

"Oh, my," said the king.
He was sad.
He liked Daniel.
But at last he said,
"Daniel, your God
will take care of you."

So they put Daniel
down, down, down
into the lion place.
Then everybody
went home.

The lions saw Daniel.
The lions heard Daniel.
The lions smelled Daniel.
But the lions didn't bite Daniel.
Do you know why?

In the morning
the king came running.
"Oh, Daniel!" he said.
"Was your God strong enough?
Could He save you
from the lions?"

And Daniel said, "YES, O king! My God sent His angel to shut the lions' mouths. They haven't hurt me at all."

Now the king
was VERY happy.
He said to his men,
"Pull Daniel up
out of the lion place!"

So they pulled Daniel
up, up, up,
out of the lion place.
They looked at his face.
They looked at his hands.
They looked at his feet.
The lions hadn't even
scratched him.

What did you learn?

God was strong enough
to take care of Daniel.
God is stronger than lions.
God is strong enough
to take care of you.

Baby Jesus and the Good News
(Matthew 1:20-21, 24; Luke 1:26-38; 2:8-18)

One day God's angel came to Mary's house.

The angel
had good news
for Mary.
He said,

"God's Son
is coming
from heaven.
You will be
His mommy."
(Wasn't THAT good news?)
"He will be
a special baby,
and—

you must name Him
JESUS."
Mary said,
"All right."
Then—

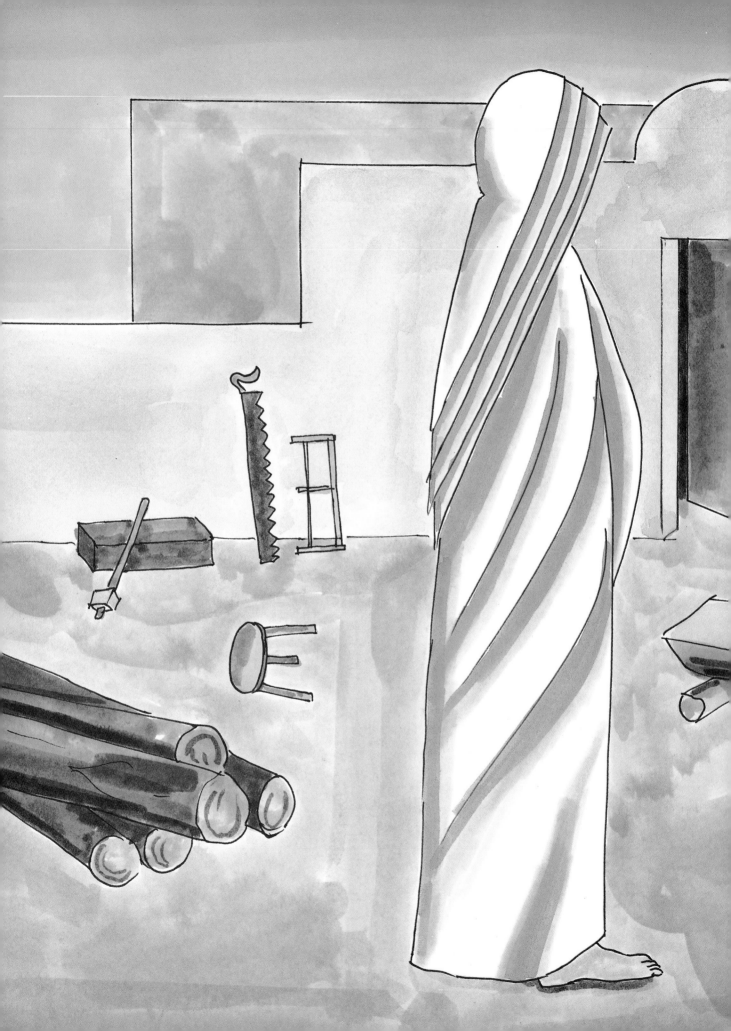

God's angel came to Joseph's house. He had good news for Joseph.

"Mary will be
a mommy,"
the angel said.
"Her baby will be
God's Son.
He is coming
to take away
people's badness."
(Wasn't THAT
good news?)

"You must name
the baby JESUS."
Joseph said,
"All right."
Then one night—

God's angel came to some men on a little hill. The men were taking care of their sheep. The angel said, "I have good news for EVERYBODY.

GOD'S SON
HAS COME
FROM HEAVEN.
He is a baby.
He is sleeping
in a manger."
(That's a box
where donkeys eat.)
All at once—

many angels were there.
In one big voice
they said good things
about God.
After that they went
back home to heaven.
Everything
was quiet again—
as quiet as could be.

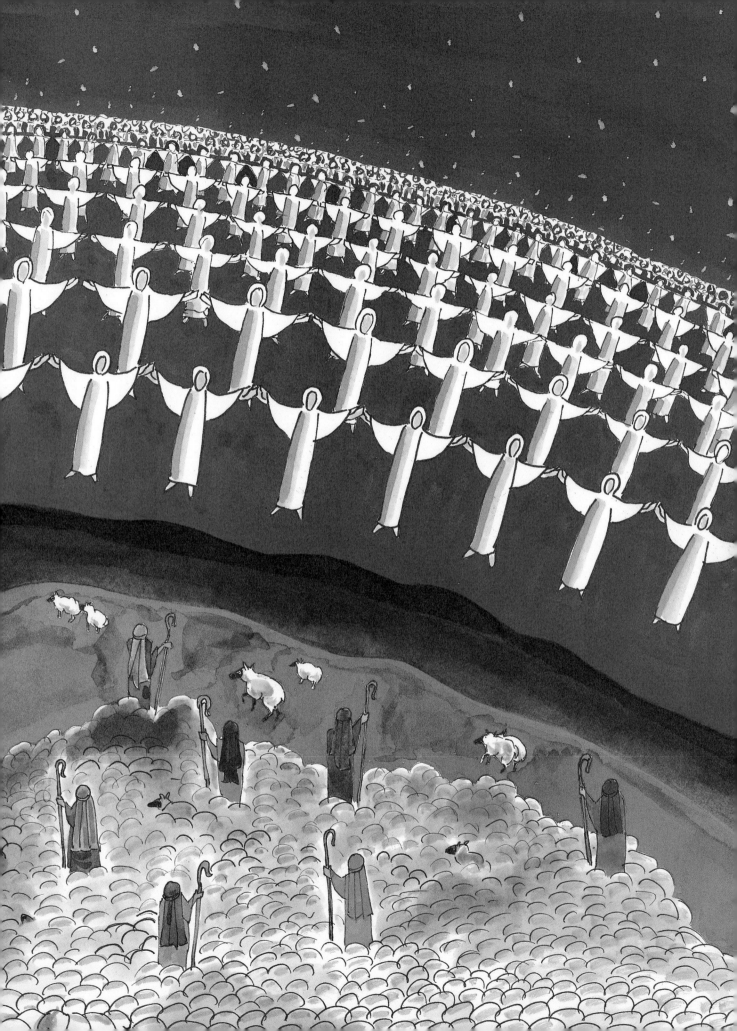

The men looked
at each other.
They said,
"What GOOD NEWS!
Let's find the baby.
Let's go right away.
Let's go fast."
Do you think
they found Him?

They found Him.
There was Mary.
There was Joseph.
And there HE was—
Baby Jesus,
God's Son from heaven—
sleeping in the
manger box.

The men looked
at the baby.
They talked to Mary.
They talked to Joseph.
Then they went back
to their sheep.
Now THEY had
good news to tell.
What was it?